GOD

IS MY

SOURCE

GLORIA COPELAND | PASTOR GEORGE PEARSONS

KENNETH COPELAND PUBLICATIONS

Unless otherwise noted, all scripture is from the *King James Version* of the Bible.

Scripture quotations marked AMPC are from *The Amplified® Bible, Classic Edition* © 1954, 1958, 1962, 1964, 1965, 1987 by The Lockman Foundation. Used by permission.

Scripture quotations marked NKJV are from the *New King James Version* © 1982 by Thomas Nelson Inc.

Scripture quotations marked NIV and NIV-84 are from *The Holy Bible, New International Version* © 1973, 1978, 1984, 2011 by Biblica Inc. Used by permission. All rights reserved worldwide.

Scripture quotations marked JBP are from the *New Testament in Modern English*, J.B. Phillips © J.B. Phillips 1958, 1959, 1960, 1972.

Scripture quotations marked NLT and NLT-96 are from the *Holy Bible, New Living Translation* © 1996, 2004 by Tyndale Charitable Trust. Used by permission of Tyndale House Publishers.

Scripture quotations marked BBE are from the *Bible in Basic English*, public domain.

Scripture quotations marked MSG are from *The Message* © 1993, 1994, 1995, 1996, 2000, 2001, 2002. Used by permission of NavPress Publishing Group.

Scripture quotations marked CEB are from the *Common English Bible®* © 2012 Common English Bible. All rights reserved.

Scripture quotations marked GNB are from the *Good News Translation* © 1992 by American Bible Society.

Scripture quotations marked *Brenton* are from English Translation of the Greek Septuagint Bible, The Translation of the Greek Old Testament Scriptures With Apocrypha; Compiled from the Translation by Sir Lancelot C.L. Brenton (Samuel Bagster and Sons Ltd., 1851), public domain.

Scripture quotations marked ESV are from *The Holy Bible, English Standard Version®* © 2001 by Crossway, a publishing ministry of Good News Publishers. Used by permission. All rights reserved.

Scripture quotations marked CEV are from the *Contemporary English Version* © 1991, 1992, 1995 by American Bible Society. Used by permission.

Scripture quotations marked KNOX are from *The Holy Bible: A Translation From the Latin Vulgate in the Light of the Hebrew and Greek Originals by Monsignor Ronald Knox.* © 1954 by Sheed & Ward Inc., New York, with the kind permission of His Eminence, The Cardinal Archbishop of Westminster, and Burns and Oates Ltd., 115 E. Armour Blvd., Kansas City, MO 64111.

Scripture #31 Prophecy delivered by Kenneth Copeland on August 7, 2009, at the 2009 Southwest Believers' Convention, Fort Worth, Texas.

Scripture #61 Excerpt by Gloria Copeland, *From Faith to Faith—A Daily Guide to Victory* (Fort Worth: Kenneth Copeland Publications, 1990), December 10.

Scripture quotations marked AMP are from The Amplified® Bible, © 2015 by The Lockman Foundation. Used by permission.

God Is My Source

ISBN 978-1-60463-312-2   30-0841

21 20 19 18 17 16   6 5 4 3 2 1

© 2016 Eagle Mountain International Church Inc. aka Kenneth Copeland Ministries

Kenneth Copeland Publications
Fort Worth, TX 76192-0001

For more information about Kenneth Copeland Ministries, visit kcm.org or call 1-800-600-7395 (U.S. only) or +1-817-852-6000.

Many people are facing overwhelming financial and provisional challenges. Most often, they approach their problems from a purely natural standpoint. Here's how it usually goes:

They look at their paycheck.

Then, they look at their need.

Impossible.

They look at their paycheck.

And then, they look back at their need.

Still impossible.

The more people engage in that vicious cycle, the more discouraged they become. That exercise in futility is usually followed by a series of questions:

"How are we *ever* going to pay for this?"

"Where will the money come from?"

"What are we going to do?"

Then comes the "bright idea" phase of the cycle:

"What family member will loan us the money?"

"Where can we get another job?"

"Have we maxed out our credit cards?"

This madness must stop, right now! We must get our eyes off our limited resources and refocus them on the real Source of our unlimited supply: ALMIGHTY GOD AND HIS WORD.

A few years ago, the Lord gave a powerful word to Kenneth Copeland. Make this word personal as you read it—as if it were spoken directly to you.

Don't look to the government for your supply.

Don't look to other people for your supply.

Pastors, don't look to your congregation for your supply.

Jesus is our Source and The WORD is our supply.

Here is the exciting part: We are not required to meet our own needs because God wants to do that for us! Isn't that good news?

It will take a commitment of time to

renew your mind to the fact that GOD is your TOTAL SOURCE OF SUPPLY, but you can do it!

That's the purpose of this book.

Read these 70 scriptures several times a day. SAY THEM and WRITE THEM, until you become fully persuaded that God is your Source in every situation. Read them OUT LOUD to yourself, to your spouse or to your family. If you run out of writing room, start your own journal and continue to watch God work for you and through you. The more you do it, the stronger your faith will become.

Before you begin your challenge, pray this prayer:

Father, these 70 scriptures are alive and active and full of power. I believe the Word of God is renewing my mind and feeding my faith. I see You as THE Source of my supply.

I believe that every need I have is

completely met, every outstanding bill is paid in full, every debt is totally removed, and I am financially liberated. I have so much left over that I am able to bless others.

Thank You for demonstrating provisional miracles in my life. In Jesus' Name I pray. Amen, so be it!

In this book, where it says SAY IT, you say it! Where it says WRITE IT, take time to prayerfully fill those parts out during your prayer time. Where it says PRAISE, lift up your voice in praise and thanksgiving to the Lord. And, where it says SEE IT, keep record of what God has done and look at it often, as a reminder of His goodness. Start reading those records of God's goodness in your life along with your scriptures. It will be a real encouragement to your faith.

Now, let's get started!

OUR SOURCE
OF SUPPLY

———— ⋘ ⋙ ————

1. 1 Corinthians 8:6 (AMPC)
"Yet for us there is [only] one God, the Father, Who is the Source of all things...."

"The source of something is its point of origin. It's the beginning place, where something can be traced back to."

—PASTOR GEORGE

2. Philippians 4:19
"But my God shall supply all your need according to his riches in glory by Christ Jesus."

"And my God will liberally supply (fill to the full) your every need according to His riches in glory in Christ Jesus" (AMPC).

"And my God will give you all you have need of from the wealth of his glory in Christ Jesus" (BBE).

"My God will liberally supply (fill to the full) [cram, furnish, satisfy, finish and complete all of your needs, employment, requirements, lack and business] according to His riches, [His money and His possessions] in glory in Christ Jesus" (AMPC/GK).

"You can be sure that God will take care of everything you need…" (MSG).

"My God will supply all that you need from his glorious resources in Christ Jesus" (JBP).

3. James 1:17

"Every good gift and every perfect gift is from above, and cometh down from the Father of lights, with whom is no variableness, neither shadow of turning."

"Every good gift and every perfect (free, large, full) gift is from above; it comes down

from the Father of all [that gives] light…"
(AMPC).

"Every good endowment that we possess and every complete gift that we have received must come from above, from the Father of all lights, with whom there is never the slightest variation or shadow of inconsistency" (JBP).

4. Deuteronomy 28:12

"The Lord shall open unto thee his good treasure, the heaven…."

"…His store-house in heaven" (BBE).

"…His own well-stocked storehouse" (CEB).

"God will throw open the doors of his sky vaults…" (MSG).

"Heaven always has a good economy. That's where we receive from. It doesn't matter what's happening on the earth. We're not receiving it from the earth. We're receiving it from heaven."

—GLORIA COPELAND

5. Psalm 121:2

"My help comes from the Lord, the Maker of heaven and earth" (NIV).

 **SAY IT!**

I want for nothing because God is my Source.

THE LORD OUR
PROVIDER

———— ❦ ————

6. Genesis 22:14

"And Abraham called the name of that place Jehovahjireh: as it is said to this day, in the mount of the Lord it shall be seen."

"So Abraham called the name of that place The Lord Will Provide. And it is said to this day, On the mount of the Lord it will be provided" (AMPC).

"Abraham named that place God-Yireh (God-Sees-to-It). That's where we get the saying, 'On the mountain of God, he sees to it'" (MSG).

Testimony of God's Supernatural Provision

Since he was little, Anthony had been believing God to attend a particular college. As his high-school years passed, he became discouraged about the expensive tuition. He started looking for less expensive schools. The Lord challenged him to kick his faith into gear and believe for his "dream school." He applied by faith and received a full-ride scholarship of over $60,000 per year. He will also receive $40,000 for flights, a computer, books and supplies.

WHAT ARE YOU BELIEVING FOR?

"And my God will liberally supply (fill to the full) your every need according to His riches in glory in Christ Jesus" (Philippians 4:19, AMPC).

Instructions: Use the space on the next page to write down all you are believing God for. Remember, you have a covenant of provision with Him (Psalm 111:5) that He will remember forever!

Date	Supernatural Provision
_____	_____
_____	_____
_____	_____
_____	_____
_____	_____
_____	_____
_____	_____
_____	_____

SAY IT!

That happens to me all the time!

THE GOODNESS
OF GOD

---

7. Psalm 31:19

"How great is your goodness, which you have stored up for those who fear you, which you bestow in the sight of men on those who take refuge in you" (NIV-84).

Great (HEB) = Abounding, abundant, exceedingly

Goodness (HEB) = Prosperity, good things, property, supply, provision; good in the widest sense of the word, good to the farthest extreme

8. Exodus 33:18–19

"And he said, 'Please, show me Your glory.' Then He said, 'I will make all My goodness pass before you, and I will proclaim the name of the Lord before you. I will be gracious to whom I will be gracious, and I will have compassion on whom I will have compassion'" (NKJV).

> **"Think about the greatest thing God could do in your life. His goodness is greater still."**
> —PASTOR GEORGE

9. Ephesians 3:20

"Now to Him Who, by (in consequence of) the [action of His] power that is at work within us, is able to [carry out His purpose and] do superabundantly, far over and above all that we [dare] ask or think [infinitely beyond our highest prayers, desires, thoughts, hopes, or dreams]" (AMPC).

10. Psalm 16:2

"…Every good thing I have comes from you" (NLT).

11. Psalm 34:8–10

"O taste and see that the Lord is good: blessed is the man that trusteth in him.

O fear the Lord, ye his saints: for there is no want to them that fear him. The young lions do lack, and suffer hunger: but they that seek the Lord shall not want any good thing."

12. Psalm 23:6

"Surely goodness and mercy shall follow me all the days of my life; and I will dwell in the house of the Lord Forever" (NKJV).

> **"God is pursuing and chasing after you with His goodness, which is His provision and supply."**
>
> —PASTOR GEORGE

13. Psalm 65:11

"You crown the year with Your goodness, and Your paths drip with abundance" (NKJV).

14. Psalm 107:8-9

"Oh, that men would give thanks to the Lord for His goodness, and for His wonderful works to the children of men! For He satisfies the longing soul, and fills the hungry soul with goodness" (NKJV).

 **SAY IT!**

I will see God's goodness in my life, daily.

THE BLESSING
MAKES US RICH

---

15. Proverbs 10:22

"The blessing of the Lord, it maketh rich, and He addeth no sorrow to it."

"It is the Lord's blessing that makes you wealthy..." (GNB).

"The blessing of the Lord is upon the head of the righteous; it enriches him, and grief of heart shall not be added to it" (BRENTON).

16. Genesis 1:27–28

"So God created man in His own image, in the image and likeness of God He created him; male and female He created them. And God blessed them and said to them, Be fruitful, multiply, and fill the earth, and subdue it [using all its vast resources in the service of God and man]; and have dominion over the fish of the sea, the birds of the air, and over every living creature that moves upon the earth" (AMPC).

> **"To BLESS actually means, 'to empower to prosper,' so, the first words Adam ever heard, the first sound that ever struck his eardrums was the sound of God's voice empowering him with the divine, creative ability to reign over the earth and make it a perfect reflection of God's best and highest will."**
>
> —KENNETH COPELAND

17. Genesis 14:22–23

"But Abram said to the king of Sodom, 'I have raised my hand to the Lord, God Most High, the Possessor of heaven and earth, that I will take nothing, from a thread to a sandal strap, and that I will not take anything that is yours, lest you should say, "I have made Abram rich"'" (NKJV).

18. Genesis 15:1
"After these things, the word of the Lord came to Abram in a vision, saying, Fear not, Abram, I am your Shield, your abundant compensation, and your reward shall be exceedingly great" (AMPC).

19. Deuteronomy 8:18
"And you shall remember the Lord your God, for it is He who gives you power to get wealth, that He may establish His covenant which He swore to your fathers, as it is this day" (NKJV).

20. 1 Timothy 6:17
"Command those who are rich in this present age not to be haughty, nor to trust in uncertain riches but in the living God, who gives us richly all things to enjoy" (NKJV).

THERE IS NO DREAM TOO BIG

or desire too small that He won't provide.

Keep on asking, and you will receive what you ask for. Keep on seeking, and you will find. Keep on knocking, and the door will be opened to you (see Matthew 7:7).

Instructions: Use the space below to write down all the areas where you need heaven's resources but have not been bold enough to ask.

Date	Supernatural Provision
_____	_____
_____	_____
_____	_____
_____	_____
_____	_____

Date	Supernatural Provision

 **SAY IT!**

*I refuse to grieve, doubt or worry.
The BLESSING of the LORD
is working for me, NOW!*

OUR SOURCE OF
EVERYTHING

───── ⋅✦⋅ ─────

21. 1 Chronicles 29:12
   "Wealth and honor come from you alone…" (NLT).

22. 1 Chronicles 29:14
   "…Everything we have has come from you, and we give you only what you first gave us!" (NLT).

23. Genesis 9:3
   "Every moving thing that lives shall be food for you. And as I gave you the green plants, I give you everything" (ESV).

24. Psalm 34:10
   "The young lions lack food and suffer

hunger, but they who seek (inquire of and require) the Lord [by right of their need and on the authority of His Word], none of them shall lack any beneficial thing" (AMPC).

25. Romans 11:36
"All things originate with Him and come from Him…" (AMPC).

26. Ephesians 1:3
"All praise to God, the Father of our Lord Jesus Christ, who has blessed us with every spiritual blessing in the heavenly realms because we are united with Christ" (NLT).

27. 2 Peter 1:3
"His divine power has given us everything we need for life and godliness through our knowledge of him who called us by his own glory and goodness" (NIV-84).

28. Psalm 62:5
"…Everything I hope for comes from Him" (MSG).

29. Psalm 23:1

"The Lord is my Shepherd [to feed, guide, and shield me], I shall not lack" (AMPC).

30. Psalm 23:5

"You prepare a feast for me in the presence of my enemies. You honor me by anointing my head with oil. My cup overflows with blessings" (NLT).

31. Ephesians 3:20

"God can do...far more than you could ever imagine or guess or request in your wildest dreams..." (MSG).

"I have plans that you have never dreamed of," saith The LORD. "They are beyond your wildest imagination. I did it just for you. Heaven is overloaded with things that I have prepared for your enjoyment, if you will simply come to that place where you just say,

'God, I am so grateful,' and give Me an opportunity."

—WORD FROM THE LORD THROUGH KENNETH COPELAND

Praise Break!

Psalm 100:4 (NLT) says, **"Enter his gates with thanksgiving; go into his courts with praise. Give thanks to him and praise his name."** Take a moment to praise and thank Him for His goodness. It does our faith good when we rejoice, and rejoicing silences the voice of the enemy (Psalm 8:2; Matthew 21:16)!

 **SAY IT!**

I shall not lack!

THE BLESSING OF
ABRAHAM

32. Deuteronomy 28:2

"And all these blessings shall come upon you and overtake you, because you obey the voice of the Lord your God" (NKJV).

33. Deuteronomy 28:3-6

"Blessed shall you be in the city, and blessed shall you be in the country. Blessed shall be the fruit of your body, the produce of your ground and the increase of your herds, the increase of your cattle and the offspring of your flocks. Blessed shall be your basket and your kneading bowl. Blessed shall you be when you come in, and blessed shall you be when you go out" (NKJV).

34. Deuteronomy 28:7

"God will defeat your enemies who attack you. They'll come at you on one road and run away on seven roads" (MSG).

35. Deuteronomy 28:8

"The Lord will guarantee a blessing on everything you do and will fill your storehouses with grain..." (NLT).

36. Deuteronomy 28:11

"The Lord shall make you have a surplus of prosperity…" (AMPC).

37. Deuteronomy 28:12

"The Lord shall open thee his good treasure, the heaven to give the rain unto thy land in his season, and to bless all the work of thine hand: and thou shalt lend unto many nations, and thou shalt not borrow."

"The Lord will open the storehouses of the skies…" (CEV).

"The Lord will open up for you his own well-stocked storehouse…" (CEB).

"God will throw open the doors of his sky vaults…" (MSG).

38. Deuteronomy 28:13-14

"And the Lord will make you the head and not the tail; you shall be above only, and not be beneath, if you heed the commandments of the Lord your God, which I command you today, and are careful to observe them. So you shall not turn aside from any of the words which I command you this day, *to* the right or the left, to go after other gods to serve them" (NKJV).

"You don't need other gods. You have Me. I am the Source of your prosperity, and I will supply every need in your life."

—YOUR HEAVENLY FATHER

 SAY IT!

I don't need any other gods.
I have God. He is the Source
of my prosperity, and
He will supply every
need in my life.

OUR COVENANT
OF PROVISION

39. 2 Chronicles 16:9

"For the eyes of the Lord run to and fro throughout the whole earth, to show Himself strong on behalf of those whose heart is loyal to Him…" (NKJV).

"God has a covenant determination and passion to find His covenant people and prosper them beyond their greatest imagination. It is an undying covenant devotion that propels Him to extend Himself to us with everything He is and with everything He has."

—PASTOR GEORGE

40. Deuteronomy 8:18

"Always remember that it is the Lord your God who gives you power to become rich, and he does it to fulfill the covenant he made with your ancestors" (NLT-96).

41. Psalm 111:5

"He has given food and provision to those who reverently and worshipfully fear Him; He will remember His covenant forever and imprint it [on His mind]" (AMPC).

> **"A covenant is an unbreakable agreement between two parties that have joined together as one to support, provide, protect and defend each other."**
>
> —PASTOR GEORGE

42. Psalm 34:10

"The young lions do lack, and suffer hunger: but they that seek the Lord shall not want any good thing."

43. Psalm 36:8

"They relish and feast on the abundance

of Your house; and You cause them to drink of the stream of Your pleasures" (AMPC).

44. Psalm 66:12

"Thou hast caused men to ride over our heads; we went through fire and through water: but thou broughtest us out into a wealthy place."

45. Psalm 68:19

"Blessed be the Lord, who daily loadeth us with benefits…."

46. Psalm 84:11

"…No good thing will he withhold from them that walk uprightly."

47. Psalm 85:12

"Yes, the Lord will give what is good, and our land will yield its increase" (AMPC).

48. Psalm 103:2

"Bless (affectionately, gratefully praise) the Lord, O my soul, and forget not [one of] all His benefits" (AMPC).

49. Psalm 107:9

"He satisfies the thirsty and fills the hungry with good things" (NIV-84).

50. Psalm 115:12–14

"The Lord hath been mindful of us: he will bless us; he will bless the house of Israel; he will bless the house of Aaron. He will bless them that fear the Lord, both small and great. The Lord shall increase you more and more, you and your children."

51. Psalm 116:12

"What will I give to the Lord [in return] for all His benefits towards me? [How can I repay Him for His precious blessings?]" (AMP).

 SAY IT!

God is determined that I be prosperous, and I am determined to do His will.

OUR INHERITANCE
IN CHRIST

---

52. Galatians 4:4-7

"But when the time had fully come, God sent his Son, born of a woman, born under law, to redeem those under law, that we might receive the full rights of sons. Because you are sons, God sent the Spirit of his Son into our hearts, the Spirit who calls out, 'Abba, Father.' So you are no longer a slave, but a son; and since you are a son...God has made you also an heir" (NIV-84).

Verse 7: "...since you are his child, everything he has belongs to you" (NLT-96).

Verse 7: "...if you are a child, you're also an heir, with complete access to the inheritance" (MSG).

Heir (GK) = One who receives an inheritance by right of birth

"We have been born again into the royal family of God. The inheritance is the full scope of God's provision that encompasses everything we will ever need."

—PASTOR GEORGE

53. Romans 8:17

"And if we are [His] children, then we are [His] heirs also: heirs of God and fellow heirs with Christ [sharing His inheritance with Him]…" (AMPC).

"…together with Christ we are heirs of God's glory" (NLT).

"When you were born again, Jesus moved in with everything He has."

—GLORIA COPELAND

54. Hebrews 1:1–2

"God, who at sundry times and in divers manners spake in time past unto the fathers by the prophets, hath in these last days spoken unto us by his Son, whom he hath appointed heir of all things, by whom also he made the worlds."

"If we are joint heirs with Jesus, and Jesus is heir of all things, that must mean we are heirs of all things, as well!"

—PASTOR GEORGE

55. Colossians 1:12

"Giving thanks unto the Father, which hath made us meet to be partakers of the inheritance of the saints in light."

"…Who has qualified and made us fit to share the portion which is the inheritance of the saints" (AMPC).

56. Proverbs 8:17–21

"I love them that love me; and those that seek me early shall find me. Riches and honour are with me; yea, durable riches and righteousness. My fruit is better than gold, yea, than fine gold; and my revenue than choice silver. I lead in the way of righteousness, in the midst of the paths of judgment: That I may cause those that love me to inherit substance; and I will fill their treasures."

Verse 21: "Those who love me inherit wealth. I will fill their treasuries" (NLT).

Verses 20-21: "I walk in the way of righteousness, along the paths of justice, bestowing wealth on those who love me and making their treasuries full" (NIV-84).

SAY IT!

I am part of God's royal family, and I am heir to the fullness of His provision.

SEEK GOD
FIRST

---

57. Matthew 6:25-32

"That is why I tell you not to worry about everyday life—whether you have enough food and drink, or enough clothes to wear. Isn't life more than food, and your body more than clothing? Look at the birds. They don't plant or harvest or store food in barns, for your heavenly Father feeds them. And aren't you far more valuable to him than they are? Can all your worries add a single moment to your life? And why worry about your clothing? Look at the lilies of the field and how they grow. They don't work or make their clothing, yet Solomon in all his glory was not dressed as beautifully as they are. And if God cares so wonderfully for wildflowers that are here today and thrown into the fire tomorrow, he will certainly care for you. Why do you have so little faith? So don't worry about these things, saying, 'What will we eat? What will we drink? What will we wear?' These things dominate the thoughts of unbelievers, but your heavenly Father already knows all your needs" (NLT).

58. Matthew 6:33

"But seek first the kingdom of God and His righteousness, and all these things shall be added to you" (NKJV).

"Seek the Kingdom of God above all else, and live righteously, and he will give you everything you need" (NLT).

"But seek (aim at and strive after) first of all His kingdom and His righteousness (His way of doing and being right), and then all these things taken together will be given you besides" (AMPC).

59. Proverbs 21:21

"He who pursues righteousness and love finds life, prosperity and honor" (NIV-84).

60. Psalm 37:4

"Delight yourself in the Lord and he will give you the desires of your heart" (NIV-84).

61. 2 Chronicles 26:5

"And he [King Uzziah] sought God in the days of Zechariah, who had understanding in the visions of God: and as long as he sought the Lord, God made him to prosper."

"Right after we got married, Ken went into a business enterprise that we thought was going to make us rich. So, I quit my job and went to work for this new company.

"Two weeks later it folded....

"We were flat broke. Unemployed. Deeply in debt. I had nowhere to go. No furniture. No nothing.

"Then one day, I picked up the Bible Ken's mother had given him for his birthday. In the front, she'd written this verse, 'Seek ye

first the kingdom of God, and his righteousness; and all these things shall be added unto you.'

"I turned and read Matthew, chapter 6. It said God cared for the birds. For the first time in my life it got into my heart that God cared where I was and what I was doing. I figured if He cared for birds, He cared for me!

"I knelt in that bare room and told Jesus that if He could do anything with my life, He could certainly have it....

"I had no idea I had just been born again.

"Two weeks later, Ken found a new job. We moved into a new, furnished apartment and bought a better car. In the midst of it all, something else happened—Ken got born again."

—GLORIA COPELAND

WHAT DO YOU NEED?

List three scriptures you will confess daily over your needs.

1.
_____

_____

_____

_____

2.
_____

_____

_____

_____

3. _____

_____

_____

_____

_____

 SAY IT!

Lord, I seek Your way of doing things. Above all else, I seek Your kingdom. Because You love me, You have given me everything I need.

BLESSED TO
BLESS

⬦❧❦⬦

62. Genesis 12:2

"And I will make of you a great nation, and I will bless you [with abundant increase of favors] and make your name famous and distinguished, and you will be a blessing [dispensing good to others]" (AMPC).

"My motivation for accumulation is distribution."

—PASTOR GEORGE

63. Zechariah 8:13

"Among the other nations, Judah and Israel became symbols of a cursed nation. But no longer! Now I will rescue you and make you both a symbol and a source of blessing..." (NLT).

"We are a source of THE BLESSING for others."

—PASTOR GEORGE

64. 1 Timothy 6:17–18

"Teach those who are rich in this world not to be proud and not to trust in their money, which is so unreliable. Their trust should be in God, who richly gives us all we need for our enjoyment. Tell them to use their money to do good. They should be rich in good works and generous to those in need, always being ready to share with others" (NLT).

65. Psalm 37:21

"The wicked borrow and do not repay, but the righteous give generously" (NIV).

66. Psalm 37:25–26

"I was young and now I am old, yet I have never seen the righteous forsaken or their children begging bread. They are always generous and lend freely; their children will be blessed" (NIV-84).

67. Luke 12:33–34

"Be generous. Give to the poor. Get yourselves a bank that can't go bankrupt, a bank in heaven far from bank robbers, safe from embezzlers, a bank you can bank on. It's obvious, isn't it? The place where your treasure is, is the place you will most want to be, and end up being" (MSG).

68. Proverbs 11:25
"A generous man will prosper; he who refreshes others will himself be refreshed" (NIV-84).

69. Galatians 6:10
"Let us practice generosity to all, while the opportunity is ours; and above all, to those who are of one family with us in the faith" (KNOX).

70. 2 Corinthians 9:6–8
"Remember this—a farmer who plants only a few seeds will get a small crop. But the one who plants generously will get a generous crop. You must each decide in your heart how much to give. And don't give reluctantly or in response to pressure. 'For

God loves a person who gives cheerfully.'
And God will generously provide all you
need. Then you will always have everything
you need and plenty left over to share with
others" (NLT).

> **"True prosperity is the ability to
> use the power of God to meet
> the needs of mankind in every
> realm of life: spirit, soul and body,
> financially and socially."**
>
> —KENNETH COPELAND

 **SAY IT!**

*My motivation
for accumulation is
distribution. I am a source
of THE BLESSING to
others, and I love to give!*

LORD, TO WHOM
or into WHAT would You like me to SOW?

Instructions: Is the Lord leading you to sow into certain people or organizations? List them below.

Date	Person or organization	Amount
____	_____	_____
____	_____	_____
____	_____	_____
____	_____	_____
____	_____	_____
____	_____	_____
____	_____	_____

Date	Person or organization	Amount
_____	_____	_____
_____	_____	_____
_____	_____	_____
_____	_____	_____
_____	_____	_____
_____	_____	_____
_____	_____	_____
_____	_____	_____
_____	_____	_____
_____	_____	_____
_____	_____	_____
_____	_____	_____

LOOK WHAT THE LORD HAS DONE!

Psalm 77:11–12

"I will remember the deeds of the Lord; yes, I will remember your miracles of long ago. I will meditate on all your works and consider all your mighty deeds" (NIV-84).

Instructions: Use the space below to log all the wonderful demonstrations of supernatural provision the Lord has blessed you with. Let these testimonies of His goodness encourage your faith as you "remember the deeds of the Lord."

Date   **Supernatural Provision**

_____   _____

_____   _____

_____   _____

Date	Supernatural Provision

Prayer for Salvation and Baptism in the Holy Spirit

———— ⊲⊳ ————

Heavenly Father, I come to You in the Name of Jesus. Your Word says, "Whosoever shall call on the name of the Lord shall be saved" (Acts 2:21). I am calling on You. I pray and ask Jesus to come into my heart and be Lord over my life according to Romans 10:9–10: "If thou shalt confess with thy mouth the Lord Jesus, and shalt believe in thine heart that God hath raised him from the dead, thou shalt be saved. For with the heart man believeth unto righteousness; and with the mouth confession is made unto salvation." I do that now. I confess that Jesus is Lord, and I believe in my heart that God raised Him from the dead.

I am now reborn! I am a Christian—a child of Almighty God! I am saved! You also said in Your Word, "If ye then, being evil, know how to give good gifts unto your children: HOW MUCH MORE shall your heavenly Father give the Holy Spirit to them that ask him?" (Luke 11:13). I'm also asking You to fill me with the Holy Spirit. Holy Spirit, rise up within me as I praise God. I fully expect to speak with other tongues as You give me the utterance (Acts 2:4). In Jesus' Name. Amen!

Begin to praise God for filling you with the Holy Spirit. Speak those words and syllables you receive—not in your own language, but the language given to you by the Holy Spirit. You have to use your own voice. God will not force you to speak. Don't be concerned with how it sounds. It is a heavenly language!

Continue with the blessing God has given you and pray in the spirit every day.

You are a born-again, Spirit-filled believer. You'll never be the same!

Find a good church that boldly preaches God's Word and obeys it. Become part of a church family who will love and care for you as you love and care for them.

We need to be connected to each other. It increases our strength in God. It's God's plan for us.

Make it a habit to watch the *Believer's Voice of Victory* television broadcast and become a doer of the Word, who is blessed in his doing (James 1:22–25).

About the Author

Gloria Copeland is a noted author and minister of the gospel whose teaching ministry is known throughout the world. Believers worldwide know her through Believers' Conventions, Victory Campaigns, magazine articles, teaching audios and videos, and the daily and Sunday *Believer's Voice of Victory* television broadcast, which she hosts with her husband, Kenneth Copeland. She is known for Healing School, which she began teaching and hosting in 1979 at KCM meetings. Gloria delivers the Word of God and the keys to victorious Christian living to millions of people every year.

Gloria is author of the New York Times best-seller, *God's Master Plan for Your Life* and *Live Long, Finish Strong*, as well as numerous other favorites, including *God's Will for You*, *Walk With God*, *God's Will Is Prosperity*, *Hidden Treasures* and *To Know Him*. She has also co-authored several books with her husband, including *Family Promises*,

Healing Promises and the best-selling daily devotionals, *From Faith to Faith* and *Pursuit of His Presence.*

She holds an honorary doctorate from Oral Roberts University. In 1994, Gloria was voted Christian Woman of the Year, an honor conferred on women whose example demonstrates outstanding Christian leadership. Gloria is also the co-founder and vice president of Kenneth Copeland Ministries in Fort Worth, Texas.

Learn more about Kenneth Copeland Ministries by visiting our website at **kcm.org**

About the Author

G

eorge Pearsons is senior pastor of Eagle Mountain International Church (EMIC), located at Kenneth Copeland Ministries near Fort Worth, Texas. However, growing up as a young artist on Cape Cod, Mass., Fort Worth was not part of his life's dream. His dream was to be in New York City.

During his second year of art school in Boston, George's dream of running a major art studio, as his father had, was replaced by another dream—the dream of becoming a pastor. Pursuing that destiny, he attended Oral Roberts University. There he met and later married Terri Copeland, the daughter of internationally known minister Kenneth Copeland.

After his first year at ORU, he moved to Fort Worth for the summer to launch the KCM art department. He never returned to ORU and eventually became director of the KCM publishing department, then executive director of the ministry.

George and Terri, who became pastors of EMIC in 1993, live in Fort Worth. Their son, Jeremy Pearsons, his wife, Sarah, and children, Justus and Jesse Grace, travel in ministry together. George and Terri's daughter, Aubrey Oaks, is a gifted vocalist who ministers frequently at EMIC and alongside her mother, traveling with her in ministry. Her husband, Cody, is a pilot. They have two daughters, Eiley and Kayelin.

George's "summer job" at KCM became a covenant connection that has spanned more than 40 years. And from his place of ministry he has become "a man of God" who is well-acquainted with the life-changing effects of both an international ministry and the local church.

Learn more about Kenneth Copeland Ministries by visiting our website at kcm.org

When the Lord first spoke to Kenneth and Gloria Copeland about starting the *Believer's Voice of Victory* magazine...

He said: *This is your seed. Give it to everyone who ever responds to your ministry, and don't ever allow anyone to pay for a subscription!*

For more than 45 years, it has been the joy of Kenneth Copeland Ministries to bring the good news to believers. Readers enjoy teaching from ministers who write from lives of living contact with God, and testimonies from believers experiencing victory through God's Word in their everyday lives.

Today, the *BVOV* magazine is mailed monthly, bringing encouragement and blessing to believers around the world. Many even use it as a ministry tool, passing it on to others who desire to know Jesus and grow in their faith!

Request your FREE subscription to the *Believer's Voice of Victory* magazine today!

Go to **freevictory.com** to subscribe online, or call us at **1-800-600-7395** (U.S. only) or **+1-817-852-6000**.

JS IS L

We're Here for You!®

Your growth in God's WORD and your victory in Jesus are at the very center of our hearts. In every way God has equipped us, we will help you deal with the issues facing you, so you can be the **victorious overcomer** He has planned for you to be.

The mission of Kenneth Copeland Ministries is about all of us growing and going together. Our prayer is that you will take full advantage of all The LORD has given us to share with you.

Wherever you are in the world, you can watch the *Believer's Voice of Victory* broadcast on television (check your local listings), the Internet at kcm.org, or our digital Roku channel.

Our website, **kcm.org**, gives you access to every resource we've developed for your victory. And, you can find contact information for our international offices in Africa, Asia, Australia, Canada, Europe, Ukraine and our headquarters in the United States.

Each office is staffed with devoted men and women, ready to serve and pray with you. You can contact the worldwide office nearest you for assistance, and you can call us for prayer at our U.S. number, +1-817-852-6000, 24 hours every day!

We encourage you to connect with us often and let us be part of your everyday walk of faith!

Jesus Is LORD!

Kenneth & Gloria Copeland

Kenneth and Gloria Copeland